NO ONE CAN DO ANYTHING WORSE TO YOU THAN YOU CAN

ALSO BY SAM PINK

The No Hellos Diet

Hurt Others

Person

The Self-Esteem Holocaust Comes Home

Frowns Need Friends Too

I Am Going to Clone Myself Then Kill the Clone and Eat It

NO ONE CAN DO ANYTHING WORSE TO YOU THAN YOU CAN

SAM PINK

Lazy Fascist Press
Portland, OR

A Lazy Fascist Original

Lazy Fascist Press
An Imprint of Eraserhead Press
205 NE Bryant Street
Portland, Oregon 97211

www.lazyfascistpress.com

ISBN: 978-1-62105-024-7

Printed in the USA.

THE MIDWEST

Walking to get my paycheck today, I expected a hand was going to come out of the gutter and grab my ankle and then two eyes would appear inside the grate, with a voice saying, "Hey, just kidding, how are you."

Many of my recent thoughts involve someone who lives in a sewer becoming an important part of my life.

Many of my recent thoughts involve someone who will never become an important part of my life.

There have been times where I've reached into a bag of trail mix and found only the broken pieces at the bottom then put my hand over my face and said, "Oh god" real slow.

There have been times I've barely avoided a lasting relationship.

Or survived a beheading because I've shrugged.

I've seen a crowd of people in my head and the whole crowd points at me, saying, "Ewww" and is then quiet.

And the quiet is always worse than the "ew."

Niceness towards others is a measure of your own insecurity.

Isn't it terrible.

To be caught being someone in front of another someone.

Do you remember how terrible that is.

I don't think you do.

(Just kidding. I mean, sometimes that's probably accurate, but I don't know.)

Congratulations on being more hurt than anyone ever.

Congratulations on evolving any hurt-flinching into a look of celebration.

You should study the evolution, and become famous by explaining it to large crowds of people.

Would that work.

Would that even fucking work.

Right now, there's at least one other person thinking about cutting someone they know in half, like a magician using a saw—only without any illusion—without any saw—and this person is someone the magician knows—and this person has taught the magician the trick.

Sometimes things are done when you say they're done—and sometimes before you even notice.

Taking the garbage out at work yesterday, I saw a piece of the Chicago skyline visible through the high fence surrounding the dumpster area.

It made a puzzle piece of buildings and empty space.

I imagined being able to plug in the piece anywhere else without anyone noticing the difference.

Yes and I imagined I wouldn't argue about being the same piece.

When I got home from work, I lay down on the stained carpet, on my back.

And watched the shadow of the ceilingfan spinning.

And it looked like some kind of winged bug that's not going anywhere.

Not going to go anywhere.

Basically, I'd love to catch someone trying to scissor my noose uninvited.

I'd love to write the invitation.

Basically, it'd be cool if dying were just shrinking into absolute gone, at a pace relative to not wanting that to happen.

And yes—if I knew I'd never get arrested for it—I'd set a random apartment building on fire as soon as I had the chance/ equipment.

That's just a little bit about myself.

All I know is, you have to imagine a piece of dynamite exploding inside your skull cavity—so you don't actually have to do it yourself.

Game over.

Feeling fake is the worst.

And the final score is the same as it started: zero to zero.

You will necessarily be liked and disliked by a certain amount of people.

And there is no need to do anything to change that amount.

Statistics.

Game over.

Hi.

Hum the same anthem to yourself when you're alone, as the one you hum to yourself when taking off the clothes of someone you don't like anymore.

And start over whenever you realize what you're doing.

The problem is not having to find a way back to the start, but thinking you have to find a way back to the start, or thinking that the start is still there.

It's like, the first person to draw a picture of a fire ended up with a picture that looked exactly like a picture of the first person trying to draw a fire and if I stop now I'll be admitting both that I'm done and that I never started.

How many times have you wanted to drown the person closest to you.

Be honest, you think about people drowning.

It's ok.

In second grade I cried because I was doing a long-division problem and there was an abnormally large remainder and my teacher leaned over my back to help me but I hid my face from her and a really big teardrop fell onto the problem and she wiped it off the page with her hand like it didn't bother her. For real though—now, I'm fucking awesome at division.

Anyway, drown yourself.

There's still plenty of time to do what doesn't need to be done.

And even more time to decide on ways for it to be done next time.

Enjoy the feeling of "next time."

"Next time" is a good feeling.

"Secret hate" is a good feeling too.

And it's not the burning that hurts when you light your head on fire, it's the smell of the shit you almost said accurately that hurts.

Fucking dare you not to care about anything.

Fucking dare you.

Global warming is good because I like playing outside.

Yes, and I hope you put your shithead-pose away for a little bit; it's getting old.

You're hated.

Apologize as offense.

And my ghost will return to begin the million-year war that is fought using only waterguns and pinches.

And if you think about it, everyone is cursed.

Everyone is cursed when they think about it.

A smiling mouth is a coffin.

And there is enough dirt to cover everyone who is living or will ever live.

And that will always be true.

You give yourself a smiling eulogy and the real you is the one who hears it dully from underground inside a wet cardboard box lined with garbagebags.

And that will always be true.

Don't think about it.

When I throw myself into the garbage I wear gloves, so I don't accidentally touch the garbage.

At the gas station last night, the guy working the register had so much greasy white armhair, that underneath the fluorescent light it looked like a time lapse video of some type of wet fungal growth on a rainforest floor somewhere. And I wanted to be transported to that rainforest—where I'd stand in place until I fully blended in.

Hopefully, youth is almost over.

Because the world looks different every time I look at it.

And so far, there's only a constant mood of suspension—a suspension of always being slightly-late to live the life that's been happening.

Hopefully, it's almost over.

Because when I distill my youth all that's left are the small enemies I've quietly imagined.

Imagined them injured in ways no one would believe.

Bernhard Goetz, get me home.

Bernhard Goetz.

My response to any crime against me is reversing the crime.

Reversing it, and increasing its painful end.

And I feel awesome.

Feel better than you do, promise.

I'm already there.

Bernhard Goetz, get me home.

I'm already there.

Today there was part of a graham cracker on the sidewalk and there were ants all over it!

And it made me realize I'd reached the last level.

And in the last level, you are given an already slightly-finished puzzle comprising infinite square-shaped pieces that you try to move around a little to complete, but only end up turning into a new picture that seems like it could never have happened from where you began.

In the last level, no one is watching you and you can do whatever you want.

But you're a terrible person, and you know it.

And at a certain level you just keep hoping you never reach the end because you don't want it to end—you keep thinking, "This can't end."

My head is empty when asked what I want.

Always feeling "maybe."

Always focused on something that soon enough won't seem important.

Always leaving the breast red from my stubble.

I do an impression of other people but I only copy the alive part.

Which is a talent.

Always maybe.

Facedown dead, I do a new salute.

And the salute looks like surrender to some.

Some people work harder on inventing ways to appear too pathetic to want to injure than they do on ways to injure.

Some pray to be invisible.

Have become invisible.

Through slowmotion wincing.

And new kinds of self-arson.

I've seen them make it look easy.

It's a bigger opportunity to fall into a hole than it is to be asked to make one.

You know that, I know that.

This sucks.

Fucking dare you to show up at my funeral.

Fucking dare you.

Fuckety fuck fuck it seems way too easy to poison an orange (syringe full of poison, duh).

I just made a list of people who are assholes and then I deleted it.

Sew together your discarded garbage-parts and make them into a robe you keep open down the middle so we can fuck whenever we need to.

Whenever we need to discard some garbage.

Fake personalities.

And no confidence.

I'd love to cut your face open with the smaller blade on a swiss army knife.

But who wouldn't!

A good method for maintaining even a little self-respect is yelling "No" in someone's face once or twice a week when asked something.

Like if someone asks you to pass them a napkin—even if the napkin is right by you—just yell, "No" in that person's face, while continuing to make eye-contact.

You have to hate others just-enough to be a better person.

You have to hate yourself just-enough for the same reason.

Getting a shirt out of my closet this morning I felt too miserable to unbutton the shirt so I just pulled down on the shirt and the plastic hanger broke.

Now I only have two hangers left.

I stood there and said, "Only two remain."

And even though I haven't thought about it too much, I'm pretty sure hangers are dumb, don't you think.

Necessary-relationships are the new fashion, don't you think.

Necessary-relationships are the new fashion—which means I'm fucking done.

I want to confuse a delivery person by ordering groceries on a weekly basis. Then whenever the delivery person arrives, I'll reach my fingers underneath the door and—using a raspy voice—I'll say, "Slip it beneath the door, my child."

This is good.

This is so good I am so happy right now.

This is my maniac youth.

And the maniac youth will never be over.

Because it is always just beginning.

27 years old and responsible enough to think being born is always an accident.

Fuck this.

Give me thirty-minutes and I'll feel completely different.

How many people have already left behind a tracing of what they were, in pursuit of some tracing of someone they half-assedly invented.

How many people found an old half-assed tracing and stepped into it, saying, "Perfect."

I want to be the kind of person who would only kill himself if given the chance to watch it.

Hung from the ceiling with a hook through my bottom jaw.

Wow.

I just remembered being eight years old and coming to a new school and mentioning to some kids that I liked to draw. They actually gasped when I said that and then they introduced me to the kid widely regarded as the best-drawer in the class and we both sat down and someone issued the challenge of drawing a turtle and we each made a drawing and I was considered the winner. It felt stupid. It felt awesome.

The most successful method for dividing people is to run through their held-hands, dividing them two by two.

Two by two, everyone becomes distance.

So get happy, motherfucker.

And get up early today, it's beautiful outside and there is even more beauty in the people you will meet and impress—so get happy motherfucker and put your hands on your own throat and think, "Almost there."

"You never smile."

"I've never seen you smile."

"How come you don't smile."

"Why don't you ever smile."

"Why are you smiling like that."

Everything is going real good though, yeah thanks.

Something's wrong when everyone likes you.

Seriously.

You're a failure if you choose an enemy outside of yourself.

You're a traitor.

And all traitors get buried young, even if they do it themselves.

You traitor.

Saying yes to something you know you can't do.

Stating facts about yourself that aren't true, you completely identify yourself.

My first reaction to not hearing from someone in a while is that s/he has discovered a good reason not to like me—a reason I'd immediately agree with if told.

And check this shit out—my main reason for not communicating is not wanting to bother someone.

Cool, dude!

Slamdunk, dude!

Because when dead, we all go to the same garbage pile—which is large and will only get larger—which is where we each get a single gold-star sticker on our heads and our heads in the pile make this constellation no one has a name for yet because first it has to stop growing—which is not going to stop growing.

Getting older means becoming more and more able to understand how other people feel and then feeling scared by it more and more.

Getting older means becoming less and less able to understand how other people feel and then feeling scared by it more and more.

I can't imagine my own face getting older.

Can't stop thinking, "This isn't for me, there is nothing here for me."

Apple juice is good but if you take a single sip of it right after waking up, it makes your breath smell extremely bad.

Whenever there's a silence between you and someone else—and you interpret the silence as unintentional—just say, "oops" then shrug, while still somehow seeming angry. And really mean it. It will help. I promise you, it will help.

I avoid things that will make me happy, because those things are the hardest to think about later.

Later is the worst.

It's time to hurt a thing that can't defend itself.

It's time to see the immense clear tendon that runs through all occurring things.

It's time to feel the worst.

If your toes are cold, put them in my hands.

If you're not sure if your toes are cold, then I don't know.

I have mistreated many people.

Watch me mumble explaining why.

Watch me not know.

When I was five, me and another kid who was five would show each other our dicks on the school bus home every day. Not sure why it happened more than once. Who knows!

But seriously I'm glad to have two hands still, because I can't choke myself effectively with one.

Glad to have two hands still, so I can beat myself up.

Kisses, baby.

Where is my underwear. I want to go.

Things that only make sense to me make the most sense.

Let me attack your family with physical violence.

Let me end all their lives.

Chicago Bulls. Chicago Blackhawks.

I dare you to share your life with anyone.

Even if by accident.

Fucking dare you.

No, don't share with anyone.

Become a tiny, plastic, nondenominational flag floating in an inch of old bathwater.

And don't share with anyone.

Even if by accident.

Because it's a bad feeling to realize you're being guarded by someone you'd never fully confess to, but that's half of any relationship.

But that's half of anything. Even if by accident.

Which means I'm through with you as a relation.

On to the goal of blending as evenly as I can with the world as material—mind no more.

And all the shapes I've seen are building the big last-shape that looks like everything altogether at once, and everyone's welcome in.

My mind is a glass square suspended in space somewhere between the sun and earth and when the sun goes through the glass, it projects all known life onto earth.

My jizz smells amazing, don't you want it on your neck.

For my contribution to the earth's death-collage, I'll be a small square of cardboard that has one mosquito leg still sticking to it from being killed by someone with a napkin.

For my contribution, I choose this face I make, which should be understood as a form of thanks that is not loud enough to hear.

For my contribution, I'm willing to mime either of the above, whenever looked at.

I encourage everyone to approach success then purposely stop right before it.

Then repeat that same action over and over, disguising it as success.

With thousands of ways to deflect others.

With no way to avoid it.

Dodge, deflect, or somehow defend.

Hurt others.

I encourage you to hurt others, and think of it as your greatest success.

"You're unnecessary," you say to yourself, turning on the faucet to brush your teeth.

"You are," you say to yourself, staring at the water in the sink.

"You're unnecessary," you say to yourself, anxious about nothing, scratching your head fiercely with both hands in the bathroom.

"You're done," you say, putting all your fingernails on the back of your head, then slowly pulling them forward into your eyebrows, standing in the bathroom, anxious about something.

"You're done," you say, looking at the floor.

"You are the floor," you say, still looking at the floor.

You begin a scream but stop it almost immediately.

My t-shirt has been on backwards for two days—only one of the days was when I hadn't yet noticed.

Possession by depressed ghost.

I'm always poisoned.

And the poisons always work because they always taste good.

Self-obsession: Important if you're at-all full of shit still.

I've won in any way you can name, and also in ways you can't.

Gladly taste-testing new poisons without making a face.

And by the time somebody reads this, I will have covered a hook with sugar and pulled a bigger uglier person out of my insides.

By the time somebody reads this, they will have proven it.

So let's finally be friends—and taste a new friend's hook.

If we start now, we can do the wrong things over and discover the new wrongs that require a start-over and if we start now we will still be too tired at some point to do what we need to do to make sure we need not another start-over but to keep going.

And the final score is zero to zero.

Everyone tried real hard, so there's nothing to be upset about.

Which means I'm going to chug a glass of my own blood and sleep for an entire day then wake up feeling like nothing will ever be special again.

Fuck this.

The sound I keep hearing is like a word that is a lot of letters that don't go together, screamed into a canyon.

Anyway, hope you're doing ok.

Yeah yeah, I mean it.

I'm all right, I'm all right.

It's almost the end of summer.

Chicago, Illinois.

2010.

4:46 a.m.

Sweating.

Cramping, sitting crosslegged in my room.

Thinking about my future—which always ends up turning into a vision of my burnt corpse in an overgrown, dandelioned backyard in the Midwest during Spring, getting eaten by a malnourished german shepherd.

The Midwest is beautiful.

YOU HEAR AMBULANCE SOUNDS AND THINK THEY ARE FOR YOU

FIRST

You are a very real person when that is what you wish you weren't most.

You avoid phone calls.

You fail in yearlong increments that shake hands with their successors when their shift is done and then go home proud.

You think that all lives are an individual's strange insistence on choosing a lifetime of last words.

You have imagined yourself standing still, smiling as everyone around you drops dead.

You have a vision of a faceless woman sitting in a chair knitting the future and it is a long photo negative of everything that happens ever.

You have bad paranoia.

You wash your face after crying so you can just say, "No, I'm just tired."

You feel fine always.

You keep putting your hands in your pockets and then inventorying the things inside because you are neurotic.

You have nice teeth.

You see old birthday cards you've kept for some reason and each one joins the swarming sharp things that make pulp of your heart.

You see your own face in the swarm of sharp things that only looks for more hearts.

You stare at the ground while scratching your face and you don't know what you are doing.

You know you should be doing something.

You just want someone you trust to cut you open to prove there is no gravel inside.

You just want to make sure.

You have seen me begging and you like it.

You admire yourself and you like it.

You hate when life reminds you it is really happening.

You are older now than you've ever been and it is not something you look forward to continuing over and over endlessly.

You are very real when that is what you wish you weren't most.

You hear ambulances sounds and think they are for you and you like it.

SECOND

You have never approved of yourself so you bother other people to do it.

You are an invisible trail of replicating statues each more fun to be around than the last.

You never help out people as much as they help you and that's the underside of something even uglier and it bothers you.

You have dumb hands.

You go to public areas and you expect people to group up and tell you you add nothing and you should leave, and you are willing to congratulate them on being right.

You don't argue.

You just ate so much cereal your stomach hurts bad.

You mention when someone else has stolen a relatively worthless pen because you have principles.

You think principles are real.

You eat things even if they aren't fully microwaved because you don't deserve any luxury.

You are the most beautiful motherfucker on the planet forever times the square root of 78,889.

You seem like a servant to someone you hope eventually asks you for something, for anything.

You get dead so slow.

You lost all your hair but I still love you.

You will feel pain.

You will not learn from it.

You will be mistreated by people, because somebody has to do it and at least you get to pick who.

You congratulate yourself on being right.

You are married to trying to defend yourself and you have soft gumlines for weapons you motherfucker.

You get preferential treatment in your own bad afterlife.

You are right to ruin yourself now so the afterlife will be a handicapped parking space.

You will not learn from it.

THIRD

You are royalty when no one asks you to explain something you just said.

You aren't sure whether you have feelings or not but that's all part of the shrug you have performed in slow motion for your entire life so far.

You will continue this shrug.

You will be rewarded.

You should hold a contest where the donations are used to pay to have a plane fly directly into my head.

You should do things on purpose.

You keep people away from you on the train because you smell bad and look weird.

You do this on purpose.

You do half of your living actions on purpose and half on accident and the accident half begins to overproduce and you like it you fucker!

You think it seems like everyone else is living some kind of life that involves ideas that exist outside your world and when you look around you think, "'No hope' is a feeling I have a lot."

You think about the why of the why and a block of ice surrounds your head.

You are getting taller and taller and sadder and sadder.

You jump off high things but always make sure to land in ways that won't hurt.

You have known the experience of dividing yourself equally among other people who only want to divide you more.

You seem all right but you will know the general habit of being avoided.

You will know my ability to avoid.

You will secretly compliment my ability to avoid.

You are proud that you can concisely and effectively tell people how to beat certain video games.

You have never said anything that I didn't hang up on my wall, I promise.

You haven't even felt a kiss yet, you motherfucker!

You are terrrible with three r's, you.

You aren't sure whether you have feelings or not but that's all part of the shrug you have performed in slow motion for your entire life so far.

You continue the shrug, waiting to hear an ambulance.

FOURTH

You have a recent fixation of imagining yourself doing a front-flip through a table and then just lying there laughing.

You laugh a lot and it hurts and you like it.

You have no sexuality at all.

You feel palpably more free when your phone isn't charged or isn't working.

You just ate a fudgesicle and it fucking dominated your taste buds and you keep repeating "fucking domination" in your head until it's senseless and it's time to go to bed already?

You are everyday and you like it.

You make friends with strangers standing on pieces of ice that are melting and you like it.

You are only bored because you hate yourself.

You only know what to do when no one is watching.

You always act like people are watching.

You are a big monster made of wet newspaper and you get pushed down every three seconds and no one's afraid of you.

You have no reason to remain alive.

You built a small dwelling in your closet with some hangers and a sheet and you did this to avoid people, not to have fun.

You never have any fun, you fucker.

You only talk to yourself.

You will not survive that one beautiful thing you discovered when you weren't even trying to look.

You would like someone to throw a shoe at you now—you would just go, "Thank you."

You miss a lot of people but it comes out as a strong miss of only one thing.

You own your own ideal and you hate it.

You should commit suicide twice.

You're older now than you've ever been and it's not something you look forward to continuing over and over endlessly.

You hear ambulance sounds and think they are for you and you like it.

FIFTH

You were only happy when you were like five or six and that's it, right.

You think there are enormous amounts of people who love you but just to be sure you don't talk to any of them.

You have weapon vocabulary.

You have weapon vocabulary but fingers too weak to work each weapon.

You are anorexic.

You starve yourself for days and then hallucinate.

You look at me if you think I won't be looking.

You look at the light patterns on your wall and you stay in bed because you are avoiding everything.

You are objectively pathetic and your sheets are dirty and how can you live like this.

You can live like this.

You live like this.

You can live like this.

You like it.

You like yourself for reasons others do not.

You don't connect with anyone.

You listen to me and that's why I keep you around.

You hate everything and you like it.

You want to die.

You never know what day it is.

You can't imagine taking your mind off anything.

You pray but you don't know it.

You get nervous the few times you're at the doctor's office because you are convinced s/he might (justifiably) hold you down and execute you for carrying some incurable disease that can't be explained but will be fatal to everyone else.

You like everyone else.

You like being alone.

You always give up when things get hard.

You have never loved anyone like it is possible for you to and you like it; you don't like it.

You will feel pain.

You will be let down.

You have no control over how clean your face feels.

You have no time to turn around and see what you've done.

You have no need to see what you've done.

You talk and all you hear is ambulance sounds and you like it.

SIXTH

You made up a game where the winner is always you.

You made friends with the walk home when you really don't want to be anywhere.

You wake up and do things over again.

You are over again.

You always impress me.

You will powerfully vomit when you realize I'm gone for good.

You will powerfully vomit when you realize it's the part that remains that hurts most, not what is gone.

You're older now than you've ever been and it's not something you look forward to continuing over and over endlessly.

You're a compassionate human and you make ambulance sounds for anyone who wants them.

SEVENTH

You think your life will be better once you learn to somersault out of bed.

You think a lot but never decide anything.

You decide to walk straight towards death with no emotion on your face and no hope to change anything.

You wear your own medical bracelets for jewelry.

You only make people upset now, what happened.

You think about what happened and think, "Of course that happened."

You are my friend and that means you will see me act strangely.

You are a stranger and that means you are my friend.

You couldn't kill me if I had a connect-the-dots over my throat (and you know I mean that as a compliment).

EIGHTH

You haven't been able to face the outside so many times you wonder what has happened in your absence.

You couldn't draw yourself if you became invisible and wanted to reappear.

You see people outside your window and you lean out the windowframe and go, "Hey, catch me ok" then jump before there is an answer.

You base your actions on whether or not they limit what you think freedom is.

You base your actions on whether or not they will result in situations you feel are embarrassing.

You can't say what you mean ever.

You prepare your home like there is going to be a big party but then you never invite anyone over and you like it.

You really don't care what other people think and it's not at all like it was when you said that but didn't mean it.

You want to mean it.

You want to know what you're talking about.

You want to know how to understand years.

You want to know something.

You want to know something?—you are a mathematical equation that begins with a bunch of meaningless signs and ends the same way but it looks like a lot has happened (and you know I mean that as a compliment).

NINTH

You think it would be cool if your hands just, like, fell apart as uncooked rice and then you didn't have hands anymore.

You think it would be cool if you never felt obliged to anyone else.

You don't know anyone else.

You think of how you would like yourself more if you had come into existence by washing up on shore somewhere.

You are not the point.

You hear ambulance sounds and think they are for you.

You think you're being punished.

You know that punishment is wrong because the punisher can always just teach (it's like, why be a dick, right?)

You know you need to be punished.

You have typical human reactions and you are relieved because you can't imagine inventing reactions for some things (you know that's a form of punishment and you accept it).

You have pressure inside your body.

You walk around your apartment and feel like you can't be comfortable if you stop moving.

You meditate on the thought of your head being a blood aquarium.

You hate other yous.

You look like everybody else.

You look gross and you like it.

You get horny in a way that feels more like sudden homicide.

You have plastic cocktail swords for teeth.

You lose your teeth so often in dreams you no longer have free time now.

You never have real relaxations.

You balance on one leg while thinking of situations to get into that cannot be escaped.

You extinguish yourself from all sides inward and it happens too slow to show.

You extinguish yourself from all sides inward and it happens too slow to notice.

You notice.

You have your own flag and it looks a lot like your slob ass.

You can't believe how well I am able to sincerely love something for a really short period of time.

You can't believe how much I owe a movie rental place for a movie

I didn't even rent.

You don't listen to me and I love it.

You see and hear terrible things and when you run diagnostics on yourself to see if it has mattered, you don't know what to look for.

You made up a reason to keep breathing and it's working.

You just put your pen into your mouth to get something out of your pocket and then when you reached to get the pen you knocked the pen up into your gums and it hurt a lot and now you taste blood.

You have a sweet pussy.

You have real feelings and I steal them.

You make me happy.

You plagiarize faces of uncontrollable worry.

You do things that later seem strangely significant.

You have no idea how much "no" there is in all things.

You have no idea how old you are now.

You're older now than you've ever been and it's not something you look forward to continuing over and over endlessly.

You hear ambulance sounds and think they are for you and you like it.

TENTH

You are upset because you can only ever control things too weak to really want.

You think "oops" is an apology.

You don't wash yourself often.

You wear the coal mascara of no-sleep.

You should spend more time with me, you should.

You like it when I say "wink wink" after saying something serious.

You like that every creator also creates by letting its creations die.

You are embarrassed by how hard you orgasm thinking about my broken legs.

You will be asleep soon and that's ok.

You are an ugly person and I care about you.

You know that caring is hurting.

You feel terrible when it's late and you realize "nothing to do" is a permanent state.

You deliberately think about terrible things that make you want to die.

You train to die without making a face.

You die without making a face.

You will be found dead.

You will be found hanged from a tree branch, twenty skinned-arms for a noose.

You will never find a branch strong enough to hang yourself.

You end up dying of old age because nothing else can kill you.

You end up dead.

You end up alone in your room talking to everyone you've ever known all at once and it sounds like ambulance sounds and you like it.

ELEVENTH

You are an expert at experiencing pain and maintaining the same look, the one that fools people who want to be fooled.

You are an expert at acting ok so you don't embarrass other people and you don't get embarrassed ever now, isn't that weird.

You make excuses for everyone and you are liked.

You make up years of your own life and you like it.

You keep backing up and the world is many folds high now.

You use names to refer to people in order to make them seem more significant.

You use everybody and feel bad about it, but even that is selfish, hmmm.

You have a feeling that you are the result of dirt slowly aggregating out of air, hmmm.

You only have friends if you think hard enough.

You only know one way to have fun.

You should have more fun, yeah.

You should be more peaceful, yeah.

You should fall down and start to smell bad and not tell anyone where to look.

You should lose weight and put it on your head until you sink far enough to feel comfort—right, you got it.

You should figure out your own way to give up, one that makes it look like you're still trying.

You can have all my shit, I don't want it.

You shoot a gun at your face and see no bullets, just a slow-growing red beam that bends when it touches your face.

You perfected a form of silence that is your own ambulance sound and you fall asleep to it.

TWELFTH

You relax by not letting anyone know how you feel.

You resent people who know how you really feel.

You solve your own problems first.

You have hurt feelings and they are sticky shreds of what was a mouth that tried to hold in a bomb.

You allow yourself to really care about things knowing they will be gone, and you justify it somehow (even though you know you only justify things you are too weak to just do).

You are fucking lame.

You are the kind of person who recites amazing facts so you seem amazing.

You are not human and this is coming from someone with self-esteem nil.

You look the way you are trying to look.

You look like you are trying to find your way out.

You're older now than you've ever been and it's not something you look forward to continuing over and over endlessly.

You hear ambulance sounds and think they are for you and you like it.

HUMAN BEINGS ARE TOYS

No time inside the sun's lifespan would allow you to train for one concentrated look of indifference from my face.

No time inside the sun's lifespan would allow me to relax this face.

I'm willing to sit in a room for decades to plan revenge on someone who accidentally bumped into me on the train.

And I'm willing to sit in a room for decades to get revenge on myself. Izzactly.

Somebody hold me upside down so only my top half is submerged in Lake Michigan—my breath will freeze it, and I'll become the popsicle stick for a large popsicle that tastes terrible.

When the goal is to taste terrible, the future is much more interesting.

No time inside the sun's lifespan would allow you to train to carry the weight of the things I only half-explained but expected you to finish.

I'm willing to be at home in the time it would take to wait for you to finish.

And I'm willing to be at home in the time it would take to wait for revenge.

Willing to get revenge on myself by making revenge a pursuit.

Izzactly. Izzactly.

In an alley walking home, looking for a rat to follow home.

On the sidewalk, handing a homeless man some hard candy I had in my pocket.

On a roof looking at the skyline, not feeling anything beautiful or hopeful, instead seeing a big sandcastle I want to kick once and ruin—only once though so the form slightly remains.

In the kitchen with the freezer door open, measuring it with a tape-measure to see if I can move in.

Outside the door to my room, hoping I can walk in and get my keys with my eyes closed so I don't have to see my stuff or anything else about me.

Outside the apartment door, holding my keys and deciding not to lock the door because I want to come back to someone sitting on the couch ready to mate.

Outside the apartment door, holding my keys and deciding not to lock the door because I want to come back to an empty apartment with a series of boxes made into a maze that leads me back out of the apartment.

Izzactly.

Amen for being a jobless outline of a human with no obligations to any of the other 6 billion people in the world who are human outlines with no obligations!

Amen for the dark gray dust on my blinds, otherwise no one would know I was here!

Amen for candy on a fishing pole otherwise I'd never catch gross pets!

Amen for me, assholes!

Amen.

No time inside the sun's lifespan would allow me to explain how happy I get sometimes.

No time inside the sun's lifespan would allow you to train to believe me.

No time inside any of this would allow me to train to do certain things over.

In the passenger side seat of a moving car with the door open, getting ready to let my feet begin to grind against the road.

In the passenger side seat of a moving car with the door open and my feet grinding against the road, turning to the person who's driving to say, "You don't need me anymore."

Smeared inside miles and miles of street-pores getting thinned down by tires.

Standing by Lake Michigan wondering if someone will pay me to keep an eye on the lake or pay me to just touch it once in a while.

Sitting on the floor in my room, knowing at best I'm a sliver in the hands of a person who's thousands of feet tall washing his/her hands in soapy water that is the combined sweat of all the times spent running around the block hoping it would create a giant hole and bring everything with it.

No.

On the couch, looking at my pants and feeling so happy they're mine and no one else's—and I've never been better dude I've never been better.

No time inside the sun's lifespan would give you permission to act like you do.

I'm willing to let everything be revenge on me.

Izzactly. Izzactly.

How are you though.

At home, wondering where my next home will be and how much I will remember to miss this one once it's somewhere I can't be.

At home, ready to start throwing the furniture out the window.

At home inside the time it would take to manufacture a way to show the whole world my asshole at the same time (there has to be a way).

At home in knowing I'll never do it.

At home inside the time it would take to train to become your best friend.

At home in knowing I'll never do it.

In the parking lot, wondering if there are enough names in the world to give to all the little rocks, wondering if I have enough time to think of names.

Anywhere else, looking at people and waiting for them to initiate a conversation.

At home inside the time it takes to manufacture a way out of a conversation.

In the bathroom with my shirt off, admiring myself in the mirror.

At the Van Buren Bridge, watching traffic go beneath me and wondering if I can jump down and run along the tops of the cars.

At the Van Buren Bridge, laughing after I imagine how I'd land on the first car and fall violently to the ground, smashed and limp.

Smashed and limp, izzactly.

No time inside the sun's lifespan would allow you to train to become this smashed and limp.

No time inside the sun's entire genealogy is long enough to measure the length of the nap I want to take, only fifteen minutes after waking up.

And shit, I give you cpr every night then wait again for your lips to be blue enough to match mine—then repeat.

And shit, somebody has to love the dunce-art of my face when it shows I forgot what I was about to say but I don't care that I forgot and that's my revenge, izzactly.

I come from the grinded-jaw of planning revenge on everyone. And also from the first look of doubt on your face, coming out newborn.

No time inside the sun's lifespan would allow you to train the muscles that died with that look of doubt.

Feeling gross.

Can't wait to slowly finish this hospital I'm building around myself—it looks really nice, it does.

Standing in the kitchen, drinking water and leaning against the sink, looking out across the tops of apartment buildings at an advertisement for cell phones on the side of a building across the street.

Setting the glass in the sink and going to bed.

Inside a room that is inside an apartment that is inside how I think about where I am, that is inside everything I look at, that is some form of saying the same thing—always saying, "Don't touch me."

Inside someone else's body as their unborn, sideways and stuck, my legs numb, with a brittle skeletal frame made of stucco.

And I've never been better.

Never been more brittle.

Achieving a level of calmness that's a crime to others.

Amen.

So cheer up.

Cheer up and don't be disappointing today.

No time inside the sun's lifespan would allow you to train to accept that you can't help some people.

So cheer up.

And don't be disappointed.

On the Brown Line train, with no one else in the car except a man using a brown paperbag for a pillow.

On the Brown Line, with just-enough energy to get home and walk to bed and fall asleep before I even fully lie down.

In line at the 7-11, feeling the people behind me staring at my neck.

In the alley behind the 7-11, eating the food I bought and feeling like the best human alive, completely serious about it.

In the alley thinking, "Yes" at a low-volume 3,482 feet towards the center of my head, which then echoes out and goes quiet by the time it reaches my face.

In the alley behind the 7-11, deciding it's time to walk home and be there.

Halfway home, deciding to live beneath a car parked on the street.

Halfway under the car parked on the street, deciding I can't fit.

All-the-way to deciding to accept whatever happens, in whatever way it happens.

At home in deciding to accept whatever happens.

At home in my room sitting on the floor moving the upper half of my body forward and backward, saying, "yes, yes" over and over.

Amen for endless life experienced every second!

Amen!

Amen for the disgust I've saved so long it can't be defended against, and amen for the people I use it to attack!

Amen for attack! Oh, I know!

Amen for the weakness of people who made attack something weak.

I come in my pants when I hear the first skull-shot of an attack.

I come from the same body whether it's the one that wants to shoot you in the skull, or the one who'd use gum to blow a bubble in the bullethole, taking you to your sky retirement.

And no time inside the sun's lifespan would allow me to word my apology right.

No time inside the sun's lifespan would allow me to get this right.

No time inside the sun's lifespan would allow me to try to make it better.

Every time I wake up there is a terrible feeling of being doomed never to love anyone.

And my lips are bloody from kissing my own ass so much.

Amen.

Izzactly.

I've been negative to myself more times than necessary and now I can deal with anything else.

Been the weakness of not wanting to attack other people.

Been alone in my room, arguing.

I've made things quiet in my room, where no one can argue.

Have made things quiet, looking out the blinds at the snow on the roof of the building next door.

Have thought about snow as a fellow person.

I come from where I will come back, because I'd rather run small circles in one place than run in a straight line seeing new things over and over.

And it's not going to stop.

It's not going to stop.

No time inside the sun's lifespan would allow me to build a replacement.

No time to try.

I want to bend my leg a way it shouldn't be bent, just to impress you.

And I don't want everyone to be ok, no. Who wants that.

Upside down on the couch, listening to the ringing in my ears.

Upside down on the couch feeling tired.

Upside down on the couch, looking out the window at the moon and its quilt-like fluorescent corona.

Facedown on the quilt that is the moon's corona, sleeping off whatever I've done to deserve sleep.

Inside the quilt of the moon's corona, where everyone goes when they die, to hold hands and keep the quilt together.

The quilt that is the moon's fluorescent corona is either what I wrap around my head in the morning to make me look pretty or what burns my hands when I try to strangle it.

And the ringing in my ears is the sound of hands trying hard to grip a neck but slipping—always slipping.

All day, the question is, "How is this ok."

"How is this the result."

Izzactly, izzactly.

At home in knowing American youth is over.

At home in knowing it's time for us to die off.

At home in knowing the fun will not happen again.

Don't be mad, just believe.

I'm willing to be a police officer around you—and to trade places whenever you want.

I'm willing to write down all the rules and sleep with my arm over them.

Willing to get revenge on people I watch from far away enough to go unseen.

To get revenge on people by staying away.

In conclusion, I'm willing to allow a picture of my corpse to be used for a commemorative plate that's sold at major retail stores.

At home, eating my own heart off a commemorative plate that has a picture of my corpse on it.

And after I get this belt off my neck, I put it around yours.

And after the belt is off your neck, it's back around mine.

And after I get the mail, I put it into the pile where all the other mail is and one day someone will find the pile and study it.

No time inside the sun's lifespan would allow the earth to create a bigger asshole than me when I'm trying to act real.

No time inside the sun's lifespan would create a big enough pause to explain why I never forget and why I never forgive.

I forgive by progressing to other things to concentrate on never forgiving.

And there will be many new decades of no forgiveness.

Izzactly.

I'ma never let it end.

I'ma keep you alive through a thousand painless deaths, to finally enjoy the last one.

Be my entire family.

Amen.

I'm willing to let my body be the wrappingpaper for a person who will be average always.

I'm willing to average out the times people have made me dumb and be the average and be made dumb again.

Living like this feels easy. Only, not at all.

No time inside the sun's lifespan would allow you to become brave enough to try to live like this.

In my room, sitting alone and looking out the window trying to remember what I was just thinking because it seems like it will change everything.

On a bench at the park, feeling two drops from a far-away sprinkler, thinking it has changed everything.

In the bathroom brushing my teeth, naked with a hand on my hip and getting ready to go to bed—getting ready to change everything.

Waking up and changing position in bed because everything is an idea I maintain by staying awake.

On the bus, sitting next to people and trying to change my hands into giant knives so I can cut my legs off and throw them at the bus driver.

Waiting for today to be done fucking someone else over so it will be my turn.

Please give me a turn.

No time inside the sun's lifespan would make me regret my turn.

And thanks.

Thanks for turning away from me when I pinch my eyes closed with my fingers and thumbs, trying to be molecule-small.

And thanks for opening your mouth on me when I expand apart— I'm hard to keep combined.

And thanks for showing me how to fall in and out of a personality and make it look like a trick.

Thanks for showing me how to be skinny and how to fall into the areas where other people's plans broke up.

And for not telling anyone else that it was me who broke up all the plans with a strong commitment to being a miserable fuck.

And for showing me what most other people are like.

Thanks for showing me the basic shape of my eventual corpse.

Thanks.

Because I never knew the sun's lifespan would let all this happen.

And I never pushed anyone to do anything—I pushed them to make them fall down and possibly get hurt.

And I never move because I'm too heavy to push.

No time inside the sun's lifespan will erase enough things to make space for me.

Fuck yourself.

What is the lowest amount of water needed to drown me.

What is the lowest amount needed, and do you carry it in your cheeks.

No time inside the sun's lifespan would give me enough baths.

I'm willing to say this to anyone I meet.

Willing to get revenge on myself by letting anyone listen.

I swear loudly inside my head, but on the outside I stay quiet.

On a concrete park bench, trying to figure out what day it is without having to ask someone who walks by.

Walking by someone on a concrete park bench and not making eye contact because it looks like s/he is about to ask something.

At home, sitting alone in the kitchen with a hand on the table and a hand on my thigh.

At home, sitting alone in the kitchen with a hand on the table and the other hand over my face as my face is piecing in a way I can't control and don't enjoy.

No time inside the sun's lifespan would allow me to train to control or enjoy it.

At home, pacing around the carpet and not finishing any thoughts.

Under the carpet is the script to my entire life and I wrote it by putting broken rocks on my feet and pacing the room.

I'm willing to read the script over and over as a form of revenge.

At home in this kind of revenge.

No time inside the sun's lifespan would allow me to train to be at home in this kind of revenge.

A SHIELD MADE OF NAPKINS

1.

AAAAAAaaaaaaaaaaaa….. (That's me falling into a pit of some kind.) …aaaaaaaaAAAAAAAAAA (That's me joining you in the pit you're in.)

2.

I still get scared of the dark but it doesn't happen as often now. When it does though, it seems a lot scarier. Like maybe if I just allowed myself to get scared more times, each time would be less scary. Huh, that's something to think about.

3.

A hurricane of knives that kills people and their relatives. No. No, a hurricane of knives that never comes into contact with anything but the ground. Be either one, but know which one you are. And yeah, all the knives still in your back, just leave them there; they make good steps. And yeah, your fingerprints are on some. Your footprints too.

4.

Some people don't polish, they scuff. Some people avoid me because I manipulate them, and it feels uncomfortable for us both when we let it happen. Feels uncomfortable when we notice we're letting it happen—but we let it happen. Making friends. It's satisfying to see some accidents happen, without ever doing anything to effect them. Equally satisfying to make them happen. To polish them when you're done making friends.

5.

The date of my birth is two my-selves grafted face to face, taking almost three decades to revolve and align into what I am now. And what I am now is facing forward and feeling faceless, wow. Keep facing forward. Keep going, keep going. North America, I hate you.

6.

Wow, the highest level of disgust is finding no difference in anything. Wow no, the best is making there be no difference. Anyway—who's in your army, and who will eventually come to mine. I want to know. No, I already know. Wink wink. Isn't it nice not to feel needed. It is.

7.

Guess what. When you work on making yourself better that just means now you're always disappointed with everyone else. You work on making yourself better, then try making everyone else better in ways that—ultimately—hurt all involved. And by then you have to start over because you've become the kind of person you want to make better. Goddamn, eww. So many shitty times. So many shitty times.

8.

Seriously though, it's very hard for me to actually enjoy anything. The real fun is in ending old fun. Or finding new fun. It's the same either way. I just want to fuck all the time.

9.

Who wins when you play hide-and-go-seek with everyone else and you don't tell anyone else you're playing? Who wins is everyone! And "Eyes-closed" is the best way to hide don't you think. Hard to admit some things, don't you think. Hide-and-go-seek is over when everyone thinks they're the ones supposed to be hiding.

10.

Sometimes it hurts when I orgasm, sometimes feels like nothing, and sometimes feels good. In conclusion, most people always keep a better version of him/herself in mind so the one they actually are is always not that good. In conclusion, you lose. Feeding yourself rust-colored shit with a small garden-shovel. Scraping off small bites with your front teeth.

11.

(Phrase-equivalent of the physical space separating one person and the person the first person won't apologize to.) (Phrase equivalent of feeding yourself rust-colored shit with a small garden shovel.) (Phrase equivalent of the smallest bite possible.) (Phrase-equivalent of a crayon drawing of a man falling backwards into his own grave giving the "thumbs-up" sign with both thumbs.)

12.

"Sleeping in tears" is a thought I have, right before thinking, "That's a dumb thought, you dummy" and the feelings equal out again. Half-undone and half-newborn.

13.

Just want to study a corpse and make cuts on it and use glue to seal the cuts so everything looks fine again. Yeah. So many shitty times. So many shitty times. This is not the first and not the last shitty time.

14.

Mate with many—and let someone else deal with the mistakes. And tell them they're honored to be allowed the duty. Mate with whatever. When was the last time you said you'd enjoy a day when it came and then just let it pass. And when last were you unable to sleep because there was something undone but you didn't know what.

15.

Sadness. There's lots to be sad about. Lots and lots. Each lot supported by a version of yourself incapable of changing the situation. (It's terrible, I know). But there's a way to accept everything you wish you could avoid, and the way is a sideways route as-yet not-attempted because it smells exactly like, "I already know." Don't let anyone interrupt your sadness.

16.

Two kinds of public death: Being completely ignored, or: Being made a cause to kill. And death is when your corpse dreams its life back in exact detail, all the way to the return point, so what.

17.

Own nothing others want. Have more than others own. And if helped, assume it's accidental.

18.

The dedication I have in avoiding my room sometimes can be compared to a scientist working on some kind of spacecraft that will be used to extract samples from a planet too far away to have a shape or name yet. The dedication others have in treating me like their room can be compared to the same kind of science. Son of a bitch.

19.

My wealth is imagined—best measured as what's been taken from another. It's tinsel I wear around my naked body, lying on some leaves, surrounded by people I treat kindly as father and hater, myself smelling perfumed by the smoke of their burning skin. And nothing and no one will interrupt the naps I take while still awake—daydreaming about a large field filling with corpses both burnt and perfumed. For the ones who hold in their histories out of spite—praise be to me, king shithead superior. Naked, with tinsel around my neck.

20.

So drunk right now on never having anyone to talk to. Drunk on backed-up ideas. Drunk on being a bully to myself with bad tension. Bad head times. Bad head times, man. Life-threatening paranoia. So what though. This bomb gets big by holding everything in, and don't you think this bomb will do a good job. This bomb will blow up stupid North America for good. For good, fuckers!

21.

(Phrase-equivalent of feeling so proud about a bomb you made, you jump into the air but then fall backwards and hit the back of your head on something and forget the phone number to the house you lived in when you were six.) (Phrase-equivalent of the face you make when you involuntarily think, "oh" in a negative way about someone.) (Phrase equivalent of the look on someone's face when they flex to refrain from saying, "oh.")

22.

Just tasted shit in my mouth for a second (not joking—it was weird).

23.

Some become new heroes because they do one thing and never try again. Others are born with bad bacteria in their mouths, poison to slow old heroes. Because not everyone will like you—so don't oppose those who don't. Just be thankful that fact was made known. It's time to punch myself in the forehead until I'm bleeding. It's time. To wrap my dick with a dollar bill and fuck it into your dry asshole. Four of my fingers in your mouth.

24.

(Phrase-equivalent of a picture of a person lying in a carpeted hallway, head smashed apart.) (Phrase-equivalent of an American flag burned into someone's back, while that someone is naked on hands and knees.)

25.

Here's a prediction of the date of my death: August 14, 2027. (If that actually happens: amazing!!!)

26.

I've been able to witness myself as a disapproving stranger before—have told myself something I wish wasn't true and then again become a stranger. It's possible to be a stranger in someone's life but still introduce yourself to that person's life over and over. Getting along is unnatural though. For real, don't be polite.

27.

How to live a life that leads to: almost comatose. How to teach someone else to live that life. Today I was petting someone's dog, and for a second I thought that a girl I liked in high school had died and come to inhabit the dog's body. Laughing. Every laugh ends up feeling forced right at the end—because the end-sound is so fake because um because you realize you're laughing.

28.

Feeling taunted all the time. At all times feeling taunted. North America, I hate you. But I can be a good wife. Can eat the steroids out of any pose. Can imagine close friends dying. Can imagine having close friends. Can imagine a myself that hasn't come to this myself. Feeling taunted all the time!!!

29.

Is there progress in this shit life or is progress the part of the orbit that is not yet realized as a return. Oh yeah, I forgot—it will be clear once I stop acting like a defensive asshole. Because trying is tiring.

30.

Hello, my new arsenal is: I'm ready to fall down, I'm done. Hello, I sneak up behind you and introduce myself. Hello, my new wardrobe is the debris of you and yours is me lying on top of you. Sometimes ewwww and sometimes eww.

31.

You decorate the area directly in front of you by looking at it—and you decorate with obstacles. Then, clearing all obstacles, you come to a clearing you'd like to decorate with all old obstacles. This is success and happiness. And you can have half, because the other half is always given back. Son of a bitch.

32.

New champion anxiety fulfillment big lifespan executive upsetting timespans gone solid. New champion isolation anti-fulfillment regiment unsuccessful friendship distinction made gold. Shit can get so bad sometimes, but the backs of dumb rivals are soft on my feet when I'm running my way across their dying bodies. New champion idiot interior gone clear and adopted.

33.

The newest kind of rolemodel looks calm while swallowing his/her sinking face. Standing still while swallowing the sinking face.

34.

Sometimes it really is the right thing to do to not get out of bed. Motherfucker, I already know, it's terrible. Too unhealthy to say no to new mornings. Not healthy enough yet. Need to get well. Need no more mornings. I'm murdered every morning. "Murdered every morning," is the shout of each new morning. Dumb generation after dumb generation. Wiping my feet on the backs of my peers. And keeping my back clean. I don't give a fuck anymore. New cleats will be fashioned from pieces of demolished skulls.

35.

(Phrase equivalent of the sound cleats make against a tile floor, when both are fashioned from demolished skulls.) (Phrase equivalent of dying twice at the same time because of how much you miss someone.) (Phrase equivalent of realizing you never miss anyone, you just feel bad sometimes being alone with a version of yourself that can't stand itself and thinks something will change that and that something is someone else.)

36.

I walked home in the rain today and there was still some snow on the ground and the rain was pushing the snow down and for some reason I couldn't stop thinking about my head just completely falling off my shoulders. And the sound it'd make when hitting the ground would be "piff" because it'd immediately become snow and get pushed back into the ground.

37.

Do you even want anything. Do you want to see me lying on the ground, breaths away from dead. Do you want to see your family die. Have you seen my version of earth, reduced to debris. And have you considered that on this debris we could sit—you as whatever you are, me as yours. Do you want to smash a grape into my ear and make my ear infected. Is that what you want.
Do you even want anything.

38.

(Phrase-equivalent of a picture of two people kissing with their mouths open, gagging.) (Phrase-equivalent of realizing you want to be somewhere else.)

39.

The kind of tired where it feels like your head is filled with hot liquid. The kind of tired where you feel happy. The kind of tired where you wake up laughing. Who wants my dick in their mouth, raise your hand. Hold it up high.

40.

It's like, at some time in the future I will look down and see that I'm wearing underwear made from a brown paperbag and it will be lovely—I won't question it, that'll just be it. It's like, it's easy to feel normal if you never think of one thing as something else. To be unafraid. And to stare mostly at the ground, even when walking around in public. And to not try any harder. Don't try any harder. Because you don't know what you want yet.

41.

Keep going, keep going. Keep yourself small enough to hide in most available faults. Keep yourself big enough to create faults when walking. Keep impressing no one.

42.

Real bosses shrink worlds by burning them. No, I mean, by forgetting them. Oops I suck. And um, it might be time to attempt a brutal homicide/suicide using a tool that will never work. Might be best to always use a tool that won't work. Might just be me but I regret my involvement in this timeline. Fucking shit. It's like, fucking shit—you know?

43.

(Phrase-equivalent of a picture someone took of someone else who didn't know the picture was being taken.) (Phrase-equivalent of the nickname for a person no one likes.) (Phrase equivalent of someone beaten to death in a parking lot.) (Phrase equivalent of the Chicago Blackhawks.)

44.

If you believe in an afterlife, kill yourself—it is good to be with what we love. Or even if you just like quiet, kill yourself—it is good to be with what we love. Find something you love and be selfish enough to want it all the time. Be selfish enough to be the kind of person who is wanted all the time.

45.

On my left foot there's a hard bump on a bone I broke a few years ago playing soccer and never got fixed. Sometimes when I touch the bump I remember that I'm never the same thing. And that I'll be the same thing when my life ends. And that life is going to end. And that life is a shield made of napkins. A mask made of napkins. A knife made of napkins. A bow and arrow made of napkins. A forcefield made of napkins. A bra made of napkins. A butt made of napkins.

46.

Watching the way a person tries to say things by moving on to saying something else is more important than listening to each try. I can make sense out of a smashed insect. Smashed insects have histories. Watching myself make sense out of smashed insects. Watching myself make moves to get people less close and I've been enjoying the tries. Or no, I've been enjoying how I don't notice the tries until later. Haha—whoa—big difference!!! Distancing people like I'm smashing insects.

47.

Sad sad futures. Sad futures introduce themselves as new ways of living—and yeah, I'd like to live each one, each time. Live each one until its end.

48.

Do you want to learn the spirit of making someone else feel at blame. Do you want me to teach you. Is it time to take out our keys and hammer them together. It is!? Time to do something with an uncertain outcome and it's always time not to argue. It is.

49.

Hey, I like to focus on the image of myself burnt to death in my bedroom, with my hands up to my face, looking handsome like always. Kisses. No sex anymore, just kissing. No kisses anymore, just nothing. And the mood is either: immediately realizing everything is awful, or: immediately realizing I'm unsure. The move from one to the other is still something that's gone when I go to grab it. Gah-damn!!!

50.

A hammock of tits. A hammock of tits and me lying on it naked, with the oil of my unwashed body for cologne. I'm getting somewhere but I'm not writing down the directions. And I expect to be joined.

51.

I see other people and wonder if they've had the exact same thoughts as me and if so, would that be better or worse than otherwise. I see other people and have no thoughts. The worst feeling is hearing someone else express a thought you wish wasn't true but have already accepted. Money. Shit. BB gun. Death. Unmarked grave in the woods.

52.

I judge other people based on how quietly they remain camouflaged—or find ways to make camouflage out of what seems like a situation where there isn't any. Or find ways to steal my future. Good thing I have no future. Good thing you want my future to be yours!!! Good things have no future. Jeez oh man.

53.

I mean, I'm trying very hard to correct the things about me I think are wrong. Trying very hard. I don't want to avoid the quiet I know I have coming. Trying very hard. But have become weak. Weak—laughing in a way that feels good to me but bad to anyone hearing it. Because trying is tiring. But yeah, everything's ok leave me alone.

54.

We're ok if we're still attractive to people we find attractive. Oh yeah!!! (I just jumped up into the air and threw both arms upward, fast.)

55.

And there's real violence in the moment directly after permanently dismissing someone from any further decision you make. There's real hope in how motionless you can remain when someone does that to you. Keep going. Keep going until it becomes an honor to look up at the person who dismissed you. Keep going until you're in love with the taste of real violence.

56.

Hooray hooray. Hooray for life. Hooray for you and me. I'm open to every person who's open to me. I can be a good wife. Feeling taunted all the time, I can be a good wife. Standing at the center of an expanding circle, endless angles looking out at sad futures I haven't lived, but want to, spinning around with my eyes closed letting it happen.

57.

Crown yourself then kill yourself. And trust that there's no tool sharper than a crown broken into pieces then taped to a stick. No one can do anything to you that's worse than what you've already thought to yourself. No one can do anything worse to you than the things you've already done. No one can do anything worse to you than you can. Sho 'nuff.

58.

Seriously, you don't know how heavy you are until nothing holds you up anymore. Heavy is good. Going from an orbit that looks like progress to just lying on the floor motionless. Not asleep and not newborn. Just motionless, lips blistered from kissing your own ass so much. So yeah, watch me salute a fucking brick wall. How I salute a brick wall is my new religion. And newness is something that—thought out fully—recoils into an always conceivably-smaller thing. I'm going to retire already long past any wins. Long past, just to make sure. Have a nice morning, afternoon, and night.

ABOUT THE AUTHOR

SAM PINK is the author of *The No Hellos Diet, Hurt Others, I Am Going to Clone Myself Then Kill the Clone and Eat It, Frowns Need Friends Too*, and the cult hit *Person*. His writing has been published widely in print and on the internet, and also in other languages. He lives in Chicago, where he plays in the band Depressed Woman.

Be his friend at impersonalelectroniccommunication.com.

Lazy Fascist Press
2012

Anatomy Courses by Blake Butler and Sean Kilpatrick

The Obese by Nick Antosca

Zombie Bake-Off by Stephen Graham Jones

Broken Piano for President by Patrick Wensink

I Am Going to Clone Myself Then Kill the Clone and Eat It
by Sam Pink

The Devil in Kansas: Three Stories for the Screen
by David Ohle

Colony Collapse by J.A. Tyler

A Pretty Mouth by Molly Tanzer

The Doom That Came to Lolcats by Douglas Lain

The Collected Works of Scott McClanahan Vol. I
by Scott McClanahan

Dodgeball High by Bradley Sands

CPSIA information can be obtained
at www.ICGtesting.com
Printed in the USA
BVOW09s1227120717

489161BV00002B/155/P